CUMBRIAN YARN

THE WOOL THAT BINDS THE COUNTY

BETH & STEVE PIPE

AMBERLEY

Acknowledgements

If we mentioned everyone who has helped us by name it would take up a whole other chapter and we're already really tight on the word count, so if you're reading this and you helped us in any way whatsoever with this book, then this is for you: Thank you – we appreciate your help so much and could not have done it without you.

First published 2025

Amberley Publishing
The Hill, Stroud
Gloucestershire, GL5 4EP

www.amberley-books.com

Copyright © Beth & Steve Pipe, 2025

The right of Beth & Steve Pipe to be identified as the Authors of this work has been asserted in accordance with the Copyright, Designs and Patents Act 1988.

ISBN 978 1 3981 1807 2 (print)
ISBN 978 1 3981 1808 9 (ebook)

All rights reserved. No part of this book may be reprinted or reproduced or utilised in any form or by any electronic, mechanical or other means, now known or hereafter invented, including photocopying and recording, or in any information storage or retrieval system, without the permission in writing from the Publishers.

British Library Cataloguing in Publication Data.
A catalogue record for this book is available from the British Library.

Typesetting by Hurix Digital, India.
Printed in Great Britain.

Contents

Introduction	4

1. The Sheep	5
2. The People	14
3. The Impact on the Landscape	23
4. The Impact on Towns	32
5. The Yarn: How Is Fleece Turned into Yarn?	41
6. The History of Hand-knitting	50
7. The History of British Wool Exports Around the World	59
8. Wool and the Communities	68
9. The Patterns	78
10. Important Mills and Farms	88

Introduction

Sheep farming and the woollen industry have shaped many parts of the UK and embedded themselves into our language. We talk about being 'on tenterhooks' or 'being fleeced', or we say that something is 'dyed in the wool', or maybe someone is 'spinning a yarn' or has 'pulled the wool over our eyes', but we never really connect these sayings to the clothes we wear or the landscape and buildings around us.

Many of us love a good murder mystery, but did you know that the origins of the word 'clue' lie in the woollen industry? In the seventeenth century the word would have been written as 'clew' and was a term used to refer to a ball of yarn. In Greek mythology, Theseus (best known for slaying the minotaur) used a 'clew' of yarn to guide him out of the labyrinth, and this led to the word being defined as: 'a fact, circumstance, or principle which, being taken hold of and followed up, leads through a maze, perplexity, difficulty, intricate investigation'. The spelling evolved to 'clue' and is now something that no murder mystery story would be complete without.

There are plenty of clues (you see what we did there?) to the woolly past of Cumbria. They are hidden in the street names, the fell tops, the rivers and the lakes, as well as in the occasional locally revered saint. In this book we follow all these fascinating yarns and weave them together to discover how the county we now know as Cumbria has been shaped by its fabulous fleecy past. It is not intended as a definitive guide, but rather a starting point, with lots of tantalising threads to follow if you want to find out more.

1

The Sheep

Many sheep of the past would have looked quite different to today's breeds, and they were highly valued for their fleece. Whereas today we have many alternatives to choose from when it comes to fabrics and food, back then they didn't, so maintaining a healthy flock would have been crucial to the livelihoods of our ancestors.

Sheep could be milked, and the wool could be spun and worn, so it made more sense to only take a small number for meat, leaving the rest to continue producing food and drink for the community.

The first domestic sheep arrived in the country around 4000 BC and would have had coats more like those we see on deer, with only a fine undercoat of wool.

The sheep may have changed, but the language of sheep has changed very little. Age names for sheep in Cumbria – a 'twinter' (two winter) and 'thrinter' (three winter) – came from our Viking ancestors and are still in common use in Iceland today. The well-known method of counting sheep – yan, tan, tethera, methera, pimp – can also be found, in only slightly varied forms, in Old Welsh, Cornish and Breton.

Back then sheep 'smits' (markings made by farmers on their sheep to show ownership) were vital. Farmers had to know the mark of every nearby farm so that sheep straying

Herdwick sheep.

across the fells could be returned to their rightful owner. Before the mid-nineteenth century the fells were far more open with sheep from different farms mingling and grazing across them.

Life was hard for the shepherds, as this quote from an elderly shepherd in W. T. Palmer's *In Lakeland Dells and Fells* (1903) shows: 'The shepherd had to remain night and day with his flock, oft in a far-off mountain basin, where for a fortnight on end he might never meet a single person... One time I was four days and five nights without rest, for first a great blizzard and then a wild rain-storm raged.'

Even today sheep farming remains a rough occupation, and one that is not for the faint-hearted. As one weary farmer put it: 'Sheep are born, then spend the rest of their lives finding new and inventive ways to die.'

The elderly shepherd above also talks about sheep possessing a strong homing instinct. On one occasion twenty Cheviot sheep were bought at a Scottish Border town; the farmer brought them home to the Lake District Fells where the sheep grazed for a few days before going missing, only to turn up a week or so later back at their original farm.

In the days before sheep dipping, the sheep were washed and although many farmers had their own wash areas on mountain streams that crossed their land, there were also public wash areas, such as the one on the Langdale Beck, behind Wainwright's Inn, in Chapel Stile. They'd even keep a boat handy in case a sheep floated too far out and needed rescuing!

The first evidence of woven fabric in the county comes from the Bronze Age. An excavation of a barrow on Bannisde Moor, near Coniston, unearthed a burial urn containing the ashes of a woman and a child, and within these ashes there was a small piece of charred, woven fabric. The wool that the fabric was created from has been matched to the Soay sheep – a small, brown breed which can now largely be found on the St Kilda group of islands off north-west Scotland.

Remains found at the Roman fort at Vindolanda show that sheep during that era were of much the same build as to Soay, but with a broader variety of colours from black through to light grey. The Romans also brought in different varieties of sheep which would have cross-bred with local breeds, giving rise to the varieties we are more familiar with today. Animal rearing would have been an important activity to provide the Romans with pelts and wool for clothing and uniforms.

When the cloth was woven it would have generally been one colour, but 'shepherd's plaid' was common, mixing lighter and darker yarns to produce a range of different checked fabrics. 'Tumming' was a process of mixing black and white yarn to produce 'self-grey', often referred to locally as 'Skiddaw grass' or, as in a famous hunting song, 'Skiddaw grey'. It is not thought that local farms dyed their yarns, even though they would have had the plants and knowledge to do so.

And that's not the only association sheep have with cloth. If a young ewe was not in good enough condition to be 'covered' by the tup, a farmer might seek out an old tweed suit at a jumble sale and create a 'clout' – a tweed chastity belt – to deter the tup's approaches.

Today Maria Benjamin at Lake District Tweed is keeping this weaving tradition alive by creating a 'tartan' for different Lake District valleys. She buys fleeces from a small group of farms who she works very closely with and has, so far, crafted Coniston, Ullswater,

Sheep washing pool, Chapel Stile.

Langdale tweed throw. (Courtesy of Maria Benjamin)

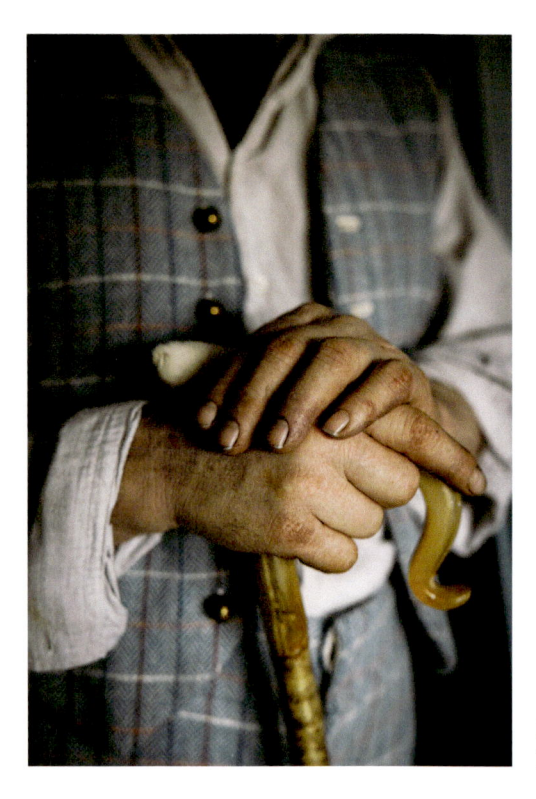

Lake District tweed. (Courtesy of Maria Benjamin)

Ennerdale, and Windermere tweeds by working with locals to design a pattern and colour scheme that reflects the individual personality of each valley. The organisation is unique in not only offering a fair price for the fleece in the first place, but also a share in the profits from the sale of items made from those fleeces.

The average weight of the fleeces varies by breed: Rough Fell, 4¼ lbs (2 kg); Swaledale, 3½ lbs (1.5 kg); and Herdwicks, 3¼ lbs (1.75 kg). And although all of the fleece can be used there are different 'cuts' that are more valuable than others; the finest wool comes from around the shoulders and neck of the sheep, with the coarsest area being on the back of the legs. There can be as many as ten different qualities of wool in one single fleece. At one time the prices fetched by these fleeces would have had a huge impact on the local famers, with everyone waiting in suspense to know whether a season had made a profit or merely a 'putting on'.

The Breeds

The three main breeds of sheep known today in the county are Swaledales, Rough Fell and Herdwicks (affectionately known as 'Herdies'). The Rough Fell and Swaledales are thought to have descended from flocks introduced into the north-east of Britain, most likely from Scandinavia as the distribution shown in the earliest sheep records roughly matches the area under the rule of Danes from the ninth to the eleventh century.

Another once popular breed of sheep became extinct in the early twentieth century. The Silverdale or Warton Crag breed were, as the name suggests, found around Silverdale, Milthorpe, Burton and Holme. The breed was known for its fine white wool, and the

Silverdale ewe.

final known pure-bred sheep were sold to a butcher around 1914/15, but the breed has been resurrected, at least partially. Whiteface Woodland sheep have been reintroduced in farms in Far Arnside and Yealand Conyers, and Kate Schofield at Farm to Yarn spins and sells the yarn from these beautiful sheep, complete with a photo on the label of the last pure bred Silverdale ewe.

Herdwicks

Herdies may be known as the smiley-faced sheep, but beneath that cheerful exterior is a core of steel. They have a well-deserved reputation as the hardiest of all the British hill sheep breeds and live in some the highest, and toughest, terrains in the UK, with around 99 per cent of all the commercial flocks found in and around the central and western Lake District fells.

Their thick, wiry fleeces mean that they can withstand the harsh winters on the fell tops, but that also means that the wool produced from them also tends to be tough and is well suited to making hardwearing carpets, insulation, bedspreads and mattresses. Herdies actually have a double fleece, with an inner 'waistcoat' base layer and an outer 'jacket' of guard hairs that don't get damaged on windy fell tops.

Herdies are well equipped to deal with whatever the weather throws at them, having a fleece that dries out quicker than other breeds after rain. They can also take most snow in their stride too – if they get caught in a drift, so long as they can breathe, they have been known to eat their own fleeces in order to survive. One account from the winter of 1946/47 comes from Side House Farm in the Langdale Valley where a sheep not only survived for six weeks under the snow, but apparently went on to produce a healthy lamb the following spring.

Herdwicks in a pen.

The fleece on the sheep will reflect the condition of the animal. In much the same way that our hair can look matted and dull when we're feeling ill, a sheep's fleece can be improved if its living conditions are improved, so although they are well suited to surviving on the high fells, Herdies that are bred and raised in the lowland areas can produce fleeces of a higher quality. Even storms, the local vegetation and geology can have an impact on the quality and appearance of the fleece.

Blood tests of Herdies have demonstrated that they originated from another breed of hairy Norse sheep, and it's possible that all the breeds share some degree of common ancestry. The name 'Herdwick' derives from the Old Norse 'Herd-vik' meaning 'sheep farm' and they have always been a hardy breed, occupying the higher fell tops around Eskdale, Wasdale, Borrowdale and Rydal.

The Herdwick breed owes much of its survival and popularity to one badly behaved rabbit. Beatrix Potter (author of *The Tale of Peter Rabbit*) became a well-respected breeder and although she is known for living at Hill Top Farm in Near Sawry, when Troutbeck Farm came to the market in 1923 she bought it and went on to raise and manage an award-winning flock of Herdwicks. She was so well respected that in 1943 she was elected the first female president of the Herdwick Sheep Breeders Association.

Rough Fell Sheep
Another of the tough hill breeds of Cumbria. It has been recognised as a distinct breed for over 150 years and although it is one of the largest mountain sheep, it's also very docile and can be long lived, often exceeding the six-year average life expectancy of a sheep.

Rough Fell sheep.

The ewes have a reputation for being excellent mothers and the breed produces a thick white fleece. Like many breeds, it was very badly hit during the 2001 foot-and-mouth epidemic and actually became endangered during that time, but it has now bounced back and numbers have stabilised. Although similar in appearance to the Swaledale, the Rough Fell has a distinctive 'Roman nose'.

Swaledales
Both male and female have distinctly curled horns, and their nose is not so solidly white as the Rough Fells. As with many sheep breeds, they are related to the Rough Fells but are now recognised as their own distinct breed. They are named after Swaledale on the Yorkshire/Cumbria boundary and the original members of the breeders' association were all farmers who lived within 7 miles of the Tan Hill Inn in Yorkshire – famous for being Britain's highest inn. The sheep produce a deeply textured yarn which remains popular with spinners and weavers for creating durable tweeds and rugs.

Other Popular Local Breeds

Texels
A tough-looking sheep that originates from the Dutch island of Texel in the middle of the North Sea. Although it only arrived in the UK in the 1970s, many flocks can be found all around Cumbria. They have a very distinctive thick-set look to them, and they produce an equally dense fleece, which is well suited to carpet making or felting.

Texel with lamb.

Jacob Sheep

As well as the popular sheep, Cumbria is also home to a wide range of rare breeds that you may come across out on the fells. One of the more interesting of these is the Jacob sheep, with their distinctive mottled fleece and impressive horns. The history of Jacob sheep can be traced all the way back to the book of Genesis in the Bible: 'Let me go through all your flocks today and remove from them every speckled or spotted sheep, every dark-coloured lamb and every spotted or speckled goat. They will be my wages.' This is the price Jacob names to stay and work for his uncle. The breed is also another great example of one saved from the brink; numbers dwindled alarmingly in the 1970s, but today around 2,000 sheep are registered every year in the Jacob Sheep Society flock book.

Bluefaced Leicester

A fine-fleeced sheep that is popular with yarn producers. The breed originated in Northumberland and is occasionally known as the Hexham Leicester. The sheep have a similar 'Roman nose' to that of the Rough Fell, but they have no wool on their head or neck and can be recognised by their prominent pointed ears.

Jacob sheep grazing.

Bluefaced Leicester.

2
The People

Over the years many things have changed with sheep farming, while many other things have remained reassuringly the same. It's fair to say that all farmers share a deep-rooted connection to the landscape and all of them have clear, passionate views about the future.

For many people, the image of a Cumbrian farm is a remote stone building nestled in amongst the soaring fells, and many farms do live up to that ideal, but there are also plenty of lowland farms with lush green pastures and soft-flowing streams. Both offer different opportunities and unique challenges for those working there.

Many flocks, Herdwicks in particular, are hefted to the landscape and have been grazing the same pastures (or 'heafs') for hundreds of years. The edges of these heafs are generally marked by sheepfolds. The flocks have developed such an attachment and knowledge of the landscape that they need less shepherding than they once did.

Over recent years a couple of things have affected this hefting. Firstly, the foot-and-mouth crisis of 2001 saw huge numbers of flocks destroyed. This wiped out in an instant centuries' worth of knowledge, with farmers struggling to rebuild their flocks long after the news cycle had moved on.

Bannisdale Valley farm.

Swaledale ewe and lambs.

Secondly, the use of 'lick'. 'Lick' is a feed supplement that often appears around the fells in large buckets. It's designed to be super tasty for sheep and offers them a boost of nitrogen that stimulates their appetite and allows them to eat better. Some research has shown that some flocks now heft to the 'lick', which is generally left in the same places throughout the year.

Shepherds

The role of shepherds has also evolved. At the start of the twentieth century, it was common for adjoining farms to club together to employ a shepherd between them. The shepherd's job changed through the seasons. In the spring they needed to collect the sheep and get to know the all the local markings. Then they had to drive them to where the best pasture was, varying the route each day to ensure the freshest grass. After that there was lambing to deal with, typically lasting about three weeks, but arguably the busiest three weeks of the year. During the summer they had to consider where the best water and shade was for the flocks and protect them from predators such as ravens and foxes, as well as watching out for smaller enemies, such as maggots and flies, before shearing season got into full swing.

Summer was also the time that flocks were sold and moved around. Sheep droving is something we rarely see today, but in the era before large trucks it was the only way to move large flocks. In *Lakeland Dells and Fells* (1903) W. T. Plamer recounts the tale of a farmer from Shap who sold 5,000 sheep to a farm that was being stocked in John o'Groats, with the sheep having to travel on hoof the whole way. The entire mission was accomplished with just two shepherds and a pack of dogs. He describes how the sheep were initially reluctant to leave their home pasture, but still all made it as far as Carlisle on the first day. The shepherds slept out with their flock through all weathers, got stopped by the police and were accused of sheep stealing near Inverness, then finally arrived – with most of the flock intact – in John o'Groats thirty-six days later.

These old drove roads can still be found around the county, and a hunt through old maps with throw up plenty of clues; for example, the Old Scotch Road through Killington can be seen on a map from 1828 as Scots Driving Road. These droving roads avoided the turnpikes of the day, which, with their hard surfaces, could damage the feet of the livestock, and shepherds were required to have a sound knowledge of the network.

One practice that remains today is raddling during the autumn. This is where the gentlemen sheep will have 'raddle' applied between his front legs; this dye will rub off on to the female sheep when he mates with her, which allows the shepherd/farmer a quick and easy way to tell which ewes have been 'covered'. They will use a different coloured dye each week to give them a rough idea of which sheep are likely to lamb when in the spring.

By winter the shepherd's job was to protect the flock from the harshest of the weather and wade in to help during storms, digging sheep out from snow drifts and rescuing them from floods.

These days the role of the shepherd has changed dramatically. Thanks to technology and modern farming methods, the typical role of the shepherd no longer exists in many places, with farmers now taking on the majority of the shepherds' traditional role.

But the farmers' role extends beyond providing food and shelter for the sheep; today they manage breeding programs, monitor the health of individual sheep, and employ sustainable practices to ensure the well-being and productivity of their animals.

Sheep and sheepdog carved shepherd's walking stick.

Farmer herding flock by quadbike.

Farming Community

It may take a village to raise a baby, but it takes a community to raise a flock, and the sheep farming community in Cumbria are a closely knit band. As the saying goes, 'if you kick one, they all limp'. Today farmers collaborate closely with each other, sharing knowledge and offering support during the most challenging times of the year.

Agricultural shows attract large numbers of curious visitors, keen to learn more about local farming methods and traditions, but at their heart most gatherings remain an important way for farmers to meet and connect. Today, of course, they can connect via the internet, or on a Zoom call, but a hundred years ago these meets held even greater significance, providing a rare opportunity for farmers to meet socially, exchange sheep that had wandered into a neighbouring flock, and enjoy traditional food, drink and sports.

One account of the annual meet on top of what is now Racecourse Hill describes a typical event. After the sheep were exchanged there would be horse racing on fell ponies – as natives to the fells they were adept at picking their way across terrain that could be hard stones one moment and soft bog the next. There used to be a shepherd's race up to the top of a nearby rock spur, as well as local wrestling, and many of these traditions are preserved in modern meets, although it's no longer just the shepherds who take part.

And what of the workers and labourers on the farm? In the days before mechanisation there was an army of them too, and pay rates were taken very seriously. A legal case from the 1960s caused a lot of interest when a farmer was accused of paying his workers too little. The reason the case was of interest was because the workers didn't want to testify against the farmer – their pay may have been too low, but it was more than compensated

Herdwick judging at the historic Eskdale Show.

Award-winning Herdwick rams at the Westmorland County Show.

Sheep shearing demonstration at the Westmorland County Show.

for by perks such as free potatoes and dairy products, which the workers did not want to endanger.

Workers would often be hired at large events, one of which took place twice a year at Burrowgate in Penrith, where farmers would peruse those available for hire, and those available for hire might be keen to find better pay or a good 'grub shop' – the role of food in retaining top farm talent cannot be underestimated. After some back and forth banter, once the deal was agreed, the farmer would hand the new worker a shilling and, according to custom, that completed the transaction.

The Evolving Role of Women on Farms

While shepherds and farms were traditionally male roles, farms could not have functioned without the women of the family. In the past, these roles were very clearly delineated, but these days there has been an evolution of roles, with many women now running successful farms, and the whole operation being shouldered by partnerships and families.

Historically, Cumbrian farmer's wives, like other farming wives across the country, were primarily responsible for domestic tasks, including cooking, cleaning, and raising children. Many of the specifics are hard to pin down because it all went undocumented for the simple reason that it was unpaid, so no invoices, record books or other paper trails exist.

It is likely that they played an integral role in managing the household, ensuring that the family was well-fed and taken care of. They would help with agricultural activities,

Seathwaite Farm, Borrowdale.

such as tending to livestock, harvesting, and preserving food and, as we shall see later, many of them provided essential income by knitting garments for sale. Their efforts were vital in maintaining the smooth running of the farm and supporting the family's livelihood.

In *Country Housewife Ladys Director* by Richard Bradley (1736) he notes:

> The art of economy is divided ... between the men and the women; the men have the most dangerous and laborious share of it in the fields, and without doors, and the women have the care and management of every business within doors, and to see after the good ordering of whatever is belonging to the house.

For those who are keen to explore this in greater depth there is an excellent paper by Nicola Verdon titled 'Farmers' Wives and the Farm Economy in England, c. 1700–1850' that can be found online.

Female children would often work in service for other farms, and it was a hard life as this account from Elizabeth Jackson in 1901 demonstrates. She went into residential service on a farm aged just thirteen and her typical day looked like this:

6 a.m.
Wake up, light the stove, wash the farm steps and help to prepare breakfast for five people, which had to be ready by 8:30 a.m.

8:30 a.m. onwards
Cleaning the rooms on the farm and preparing for lunch, which had to be ready by 12:30 p.m.

4 p.m.
Afternoon tea, which Elizabeth needed to prepare in between washing floors.

8 p.m.
Prepare and serve supper before finally finishing.

She would do this for six months of the year before returning home again in time for haymaking.

As farming practices evolved, Cumbrian farmer's wives faced new challenges and opportunities. Economic pressures and the need for diversification prompted many women to actively contribute to the farm's operations beyond domestic tasks. In Chapter 6 we explore how knitting enabled them to make an invaluable contribution to the household income, but it was this reliance on knitting that meant that the women were hit particularly hard by the Industrial Revolution when it removed that stream of income from small rural areas.

As the farms themselves evolved, the women became more involved in decision-making processes, supporting the financial management of the farm, marketing, and diversifying income streams by taking in guests on a B&B or holiday let basis. Some took on opening and managing farm shops or exploring agritourism ventures as a way to generate revenue for farms which could no longer rely on the sale of fleeces to support them.

Women farmers.

Today, women have emerged as influential advocates and farming community leaders. They have first-hand experiences of all aspects of agricultural operations and are passionate voices for rural issues.

Today's Biggest Challenge

One area that has come to the fore over recent years it the issue of mental health. As with many traditionally masculine-dominated industries, providing a safe space for farmers to open up has been challenging. Several studies have found that farmers are at an increased risk of mental illness, often due to the isolated nature of their roles and lack of specific support available.

Farming has changed radically over the past few decades and many farms have recently seen their income streams fluctuate wildly or drop dramatically, with a succession of crises rolling in one after the other including foot and mouth, Brexit, and Covid.

Organisations such as the Farming Community Network exist to support farmers, and their families, when they need it most. There is no doubt that although roles on a farm may have evolved over the generations, at the heart of it all remains the need for a strong and supportive community.

Farmer and sheepdog herding in all weathers.

3
The Impact on the Landscape

This is perhaps the trickiest, and certainly the most contentious chapter to tackle, so the aim is to keep it as factual as possible. The first thing to bear in mind is that sheep don't farm themselves so, despite all the talk about 'sheep destroying the landscape', as if it's a wilful decision on the part of the sheep, it could perhaps be better reframed as 'how the human desire to farm sheep, for whatever reason, has impacted the landscape'.

It's also an ongoing argument that will never be resolved to everyone's satisfaction. The more we have involved ourselves with wildlife projects, the more we see how the aims and objectives for one group trying to protect one thing can clash with the aims and objectives of another group trying to protect something else.

The plan was to start with some historical facts about how land use and sheep numbers have changed over the years, but even that's not straightforward because up until 1974 data was collected for Cumberland, Westmorland, and Lancashire, which obviously doesn't match modern Cumbrian boundaries, so we can't directly compare. We decided to take the data for Cumberland and Westmorland and compare that with East and West Cumbria today – it's not perfect, but it does still give us an interesting picture.

High Street.

Langdale Herdwick flock.

Year	Total Sheep
1905	957,596 (Cumberland & Westmorland)
1950	990,006 (Cumberland & Westmorland)
2000	2,633,973 (East Cumbria & West Cumbria)
2021	2,007,849 (East Cumbria & West Cumbria)

The dramatic change in numbers is largely down to dramatic changes in subsidies and funding for farms during the late twentieth and early twenty-first centuries.

Sheep farming was at the heart of the bid for UNESCO World Heritage Status, which was achieved in July 2017. The sheep were specifically part of the section on Outstanding Universal Value, which UNESCO define as: 'cultural and/or natural significance which is so exceptional as to transcend national boundaries and to be of common importance for present and future generations of all humanity.' In a nutshell, the sheep, and sheep farming, were recognised as being a crucial element of what makes the Lake District landscape unique.

Overgrazing

The argument against these high numbers of sheep is that they overgraze the landscape, creating problems for other wildlife. This overgrazing means that habitats for ground-nesting birds are destroyed, hillsides are left bare of vegetation resulting in greater erosion, and rare species of plants are nibbled out of existence. George Monbiot is almost singlehandedly responsible for bringing this into the public eye with his infamous 'Sheepwrecked' article from *The Spectator* in 2013. Dramatic as that article was, there's

Sheep pen, Tilberthwaite.

not getting away from the fact that 2 million sheep (2021 numbers) will have a greater impact on the landscape than just under 1 million sheep (1905 numbers).

The University of Liverpool set out to explore if, and how, sheep grazing impacts the landscape and their reports from 2020 makes for interesting reading. They aimed to answer the question by undertaking a series of long-term ecological experiments to analyse the vegetation – some of the experiments were initially set up in the 1950s and have been producing data since the Lake District first achieved National Park status.

All the experiments took place on two adjacent pieces of land, one that had been used for grazing sheep, and one that had not. The team tested leaf properties of seven species and their findings, published in the *Annals of Applied Biology* showed that the vegetation from the ungrazed plot was more nutritious and digestible that the vegetation in the grazed plot.

One of the leaders of the study, Professor Rob Marrs, commented: 'Our findings confirm that the 'white woolly maggots' have indeed eaten at least some of the heart out of the uplands. With the reduction or removal of sheep these landscapes can recover, but our long-term monitoring showed it can take up to 60 years for these focal species to increase.'

Removing the sheep is a brutal and possibly over-simplistic response to a farming tradition that has defined the landscape for thousands of years and has, unsurprisingly, provoked a heated response from many farmers – who of us wouldn't feel aggrieved if our way of life came under public scrutiny, inviting negative comments from those who know little about what we do?

Upland dry-stone walls.

Even those organisations whose specific role it is to protect and preserve the landscape – the National Trust and the Lake District National Park Authority – have come under fire for actions they have taken.

Rewilding

One term that is used a lot these days is 'rewilding', and its main aim is to reduce the human influence and impact on the landscape. The problem is that, when it comes to sheep farming, the farms have been there for generations. As such, many farmers feel that rewilding is a direct attack on their way of life and is aiming to eliminate them from the landscape they love.

Other concerns about rewilding include a fear that management of the land is being taken away from those who are local and have lived there for generations, and handed to unknown, and untrusted, external organisations, or that it involves returning to a rose-tinted view of the past and how things were, instead of seeking to create something new for the future.

Clearly something needs to change. Just because something has happened in one way for a long period of time doesn't mean it can't, or shouldn't, change, and it's wrong to suggest that farming methods and traditions have remained unchanged over the centuries. In *In Lakeland Dells and Fells* from 1903, W. T. Palmer recounts a conversation with an 'old-time shepherd' who recalls, 'You know that dale, eh? I well remember the time when all the high fells you can see from it were open and common to its farmers. Now they are cut up according to the size of the holdings.' He goes on to describe how every farm had the right to send a set number of sheep to graze on the fells.

He also talks about another issue that's still prevalent today: the concern that sheep, and lambs in particular, are predated by local wildlife. This is something that's explored

Crook Pinfold, enclosure for strayed livestock.

in detail in the excellent 2023 film *The Eagle with the Sunlit Eye* and, although this documentary is set in Scotland, it has many themes that will be of concern to Cumbrian farmers. The 'old-time shepherd' cites ravens and foxes as the main enemy and comments that 'hawks, magpies and carrion crows do not do a fraction of harm to living sheep or lambs'.

Haweswater

It's fair to say that clear communication, trust and a partnership approach are what's needed to tackle this hugely complex issue. One area where some progress is being made is around Haweswater, where the RSPB and Lee Schofield are working together with local farmers to try and improve the valley for everyone.

The backstory is that the RSPB took over ownership and management of Naddle and Swindale farms in 2012 and set out to prove that hill farming could be compatible with nature recovery. Swindale Valley is a beautiful spot, culminating in a stunning waterfall at the head of the valley that would be a hotspot tourist attraction if it wasn't quite so far off the beaten track.

Despite having a background in conservation management, Lee did ponder if he'd bitten off more than he could chew with this project and his book *Wild Fell* tells the story in great detail. He was an outsider in the eyes of the local farmers and needed to build trust before they could work together productively, but he remained focused on the fact that this was something that would only work if it was 'done with' not 'done to' the local famers.

The aims of the project were modest and they were clear that they never wanted to remove the sheep, but rather to reduce the numbers so that everything would be more balanced.

Swindale Beck Waterfall.

They also wanted to 'rewiggle' Swindale Beck to improve the biodiversity in the water and prevent flooding further downstream. The beck had originally been straightened to make better use of nearby land for farming.

It's a testament to their approach that many visitors are a little disappointed that there's not been more of a dramatic change, and that's the whole point: it didn't need a dramatic change, it needed a lot of smaller tweaks.

One addition has been the planting of juniper – popular with gin drinkers, although not grown in Cumbria in large enough volumes to support the gin industry. Juniper will grow, very slowly, on a whole variety of different soils. It takes two winters to germinate, but the bushes can live to around 250 years.

Because it grows low to the ground and because it's the last thing the sheep will eat, other native species such as willow, ash and birch seed within it and grow up through it. It also makes for a handy shelter for sheep too during bad weather.

A study by South Lakes Ecology demonstrated that over forty different species relied solely on juniper for their survival, and for dozens more it was a vital part of their diet, so it's also a crucial part of our nation's ecology and the reason that replanting is such an important issue.

The 'rewiggling' of the beck was one of the biggest projects undertaken and allowing it to revert to its natural course wasn't easy, but it has already resulted in salmon returning

Swindale Head.

Swindale Head Farm.

to the valley for the first time in recent memory. The newly re-added bends slow the water flow and allow eggs to be laid and hatch. There has been a noticeable increase in other wildlife too, including otters.

It wasn't just local sheep farmers that Lee needed to work with, he also had to convince local interest groups about the necessity of fencing to improve and maintain the landscape, a task made harder by the UNESCO World Heritage status and the additional requirements that brought with it.

It's a journey that has come a long way, and it's also a journey that's far from over. There's no 'Mills & Boon' ending where everyone wanders off hand in hand into the sunset, but they have come to an understanding with most local farmers and many are now working together, building on the improvements they have already seen.

Much of the future of the project is reliant on government funding schemes, but the good news is that others have been spurred on by the successes the team have achieved, and similar projects are now underway in other parts of the county.

Swindale Beck 'rewiggling'.

Swindale Valley.

4
The Impact on Towns

The wool trade has left its mark across most towns and villages in the county, from streets such as Carding Mill Lane in Keswick, to modern house names like 'Woolbarn' and 'The Yan', etc.

Sheep also left their mark on place names too: Wetheral, comes from 'corner where sheep are kept' and Soutergate means 'sheep road'. The reason for the difference in the names is because Wetherall comes from Old English, whereas Soutergate comes from Old Norse. Then there's Gimmer Crag, which comes from the local Cumbrian dialect for a young ewe.

But there are also some that can fool you. Ewedale and Woolden, for example, both come from the old words for 'wolfs' valley' and have nothing at all to do with sheep – again, the difference is that Ewedale is derived from Old Norse and Woolden from Old English.

There are many other examples, but rather than dart all over the county we are instead taking a wool tour of the town at the heart of the woollen trade, Kendal. By exploring the telltale signs of the wool trade on the buildings here you can 'get your eye in' for similar features seen elsewhere.

Carding Mill Lane, Keswick.

For much of the research here we are indebted to John Satchell and his excellent books *Kendal on Tenterhooks* and *The Kendal Weaver* – both well worth a read if you want to dig much deeper into the woolly past of the town.

Kendal's economic development was primarily driven by the wool trade. It was the perfect location: near to the sheep-grazing fells, right on the river, and with excellent transportation routes, which were then improved and extended as the town grew. Nether Bridge was on the main route from Kendal to London and in 1376 Edward III granted the right to charge a toll over the bridge to support its upkeep. Crossing it today you can still step into the recesses that were originally created to allow pedestrians to avoid passing packhorses.

In the Beginning

The first cloths produced here would have been rough cloths for working people and there are records of these as far back as 1390 when Richard II mentioned 'Kendal Cloth' and, in 1398, Henry IV granted a three-year tax concession on it.

This trade offered great employment opportunities for the local population. Most people in and around Kendal were involved in the wool trade in one way or another, including sheep farming, shearing, spinning, weaving, and dyeing. John Speed's map

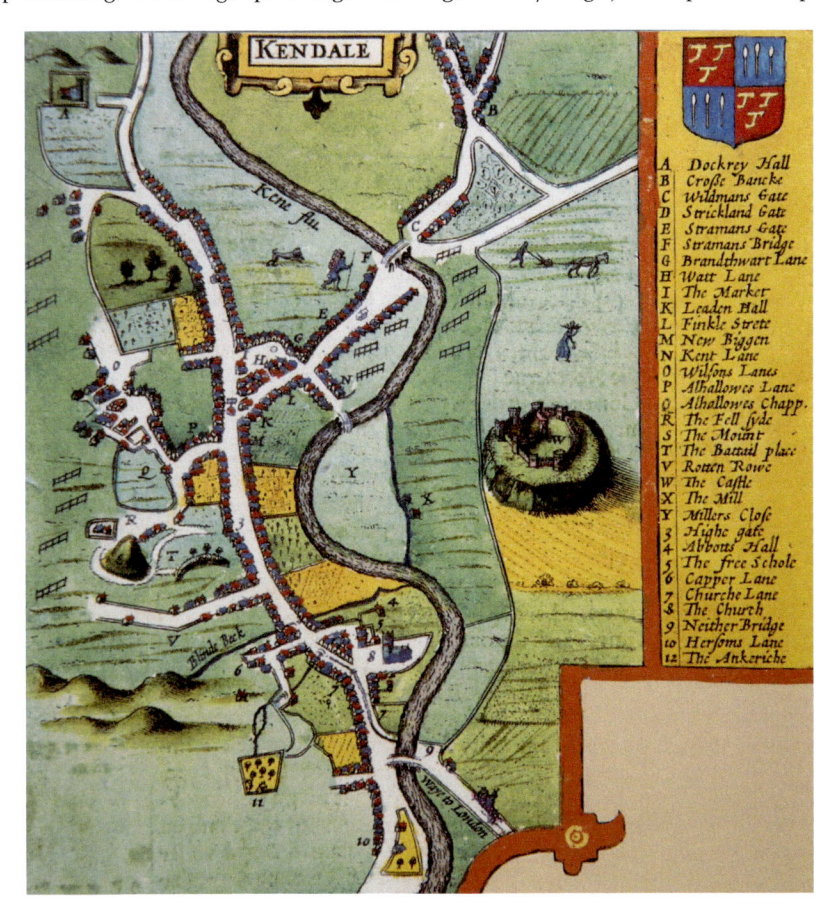

John Speed's map of Kendal, 1610.

from 1610 shows the extent of the impact of the industry on the town and his commentary includes:

> This Town is of great trade and resort, and for the diligent and industrious practise of making cloth so excels the rest, that in regard thereof it carrieth a super-eminent name above them, and hath great vent and traffick for her woollen Cloaths through all the parts of England.

Lady Anne Clifford, a formidable and iconic woman of her time, provides the first concrete evidence of fine cloth, as opposed to rougher fabrics, being sold in Kendal, with her account book from 1673 documenting a payment to George Sedgwick for 'fine Scarlett Cloth ... which he bought for me at Kendal to give away'.

As the wool trade flourished, Kendal attracted merchants, traders, and craftsmen involved in the industry. The town's infrastructure and buildings developed to support the woollen trade with the construction of warehouses, mills, and workshops. The growth of the wool industry also led to the establishment of markets and fairs.

Wealthy wool merchants and traders became prominent figures in the community, with their names enshrined in the streets and buildings of the town as they accumulated great wealth and influence.

The production of unique woollen textiles, such as Kendal Green, became synonymous with the town and Kendal's association with wool, and the craftsmanship involved in its production, contributed to the local identity and cultural heritage of the town.

The ten sites we have covered in this chapter provides real feel for the history of the town and how it evolved.

Kendal Museum

A visit to Kendal Museum is always a great idea but, but before you head through the doors, take a moment to look at the outside of the building.

This was once known as Albert Buildings and was home to the wool auction warehouse of Whitwell and Hargreaves. The company was originally founded in Lowther Street in 1857 but moved to this site in 1864. If you look on a map, you'll notice that Kendal town railway station is nearby, and a siding used to run from here, directly into the warehouse.

Kendal Museum was founded in 1796 and, following some financial difficulties, the Town Council offered them use of Albert Buildings in 1913 and they moved in after the end of the First World War.

No. 11 Stramongate

Little remains of this spinning history gem, but if you look closely you can still spot the ancient indicators in the modern café frontage.

In the early part of the nineteenth century many of the houses in the town had their own spinning galleries, which were balcony like extensions on the first floor of the properties, tucked up under the eaves, that allowed the occupants space to dry, spin, knit and store yarn in the shade. They would even have been used as display areas to sell any items made.

Kendal Museum.

Often, the space underneath the gallery would have been used for shearing and washing the yarn. These spaces were known as 'undercrofts' and it's still common today for local 'upside down' homes built into hillsides to call the downstairs area an 'undercroft'.

Sheep-washing Steps

These are tricky to pick out, but as you walk along the river keep looking down along the wall and you'll soon spot them. They are simply a flight of small stone steps leading down to the river and would have allowed people to wash sheep, fleeces, fabrics, and yarns. There used to be many more of them than there are today, but they have been lost over the years due to development and regular floods.

Bishops Court

Bishop Blaise is the patron saint of sufferers of sore throats. Legend tells us that he removed a fishbone from the throat of a small boy, saving him from certain death. The wool combers' guilds adopted him as their patron saint as they were particularly susceptible to sore throats thanks to the environments they worked in. Long before the days of Health and Safety the air would have been thick with coal fumes and wool dust.

The Feast of St Blaise was celebrated each year with a huge procession from Stramongate, along the river and down Sandes close (see Chapter 8 for more detail).

Sandes Hospital Cottages

Thomas Sandes founded the hospital for poor widows, and the coat of arms above the entrance, replete with yarn-processing tools, gives an indication of where his wealth came from. The women could live in the cottages, rent free, and received a shilling a week for carding, spinning and weaving fleeces supplied by Thomas.

Sandes Hospital coat of arms.

Note the difference between the two bats on the left: the top one is a carding bat, but the lower one is a friezing bat which was used to make a fabric known as 'frieze'. The surface of this fabric was hand brushed with a 'frieze bat' made of wild teasel heads.

As well as holding the role of Mayor of Kendal in 1647/48, he was a member of the powerful Shearman Dyers Company, and he founded the hospital in 1670. There is also a rather splendid marble memorial to him in the parish church.

The Horse and Rainbow Pub

The Horse and Rainbow is one of many old inns in Kendal. It is first mentioned in the Annals of Kendal in 1648 and has gone through several name changes over the years: The Rainbow Tavern, Pot of Gold, and Mrs Lawsons.

Rainbow is an unusual name from a pub, but it comes from the fact that a dove and rainbow were the traditional symbols of the fabric dyers' trade, and this part of town was once home to many dyers as we see from the next location.

The Old Dye Works

Another impressive old pub marks the entrance to the next location. Just to the right of Ye Olde Fleece Inn is a small passageway that leads to Old Shambles Yard, and at the head of the yard is a building that was once home to Whitaker's Dye Works.

The company was founded by Joseph Whitaker in 1879, and he moved to this building around 1895. He described himself as a 'dye merchant' and the building became known locally as 'The Colour Works'. Old dye bottles, some still containing dye, can still be found on popular internet trading sites.

Above left: The Horse and Rainbow pub.

Above right: The Old Dye Works.

Woolpack Arch
Clearly the name is a huge clue to the woolly past of this part of town, but there's more to it than that. The arch was once part of The Woolpack Inn, a popular stop on local trading routes. The popularity of the wool trade in Kendal meant that it became an important hub on the new turnpike roads system, something that greatly benefits the town to this day as many modern roads were built on these routes.

But the roads weren't quite so good back then. In a survey from 1730 all the roads were described as poor or (rather delightfully) 'covered with ye hedges'. Such was the strategic importance of the town for trading, all the roads were subsequently reinforced, and the arch at The Woolpack was rebuilt in 1791 to raise its height so that fully loaded stage wagons could pass through it. Sadly, the inn itself closed in 1997, but the wonderful arch remains.

The Working Men's Institute
This impressive building in the top corner of Branthwaite Brow is ignored by many, but it has a long and intriguing past. In 1636 it was bought by the town's mayor (Thomas Sledall) for £20 and it was used as a weighing loft where locally produced yarn was weighed out ready for sale to the garment manufacturers. By 1758 it had been refurbished and extended to become a Kendal's first theatre and by 1843 it had become the Working Man's Reading Association.

Woolpack Arch.

The Working Men's Institute.

As a sidenote, the building next door (now a café) is the site of the old Football Inn and is one of the oldest football-related buildings in England, with records dating back to 1774. There's also an excellent yarn shop, Coolcrafting, that can be found a few doors down from the institute.

The Kent Carpet Factory

The Industrial Revolution had a significant impact on Kendal, with mechanisation completely changing not only the way that garments were produced, but also the buildings in which they were made. This meant that processes that had previous taken place in smaller homes or purpose-built accommodation now required much larger buildings to house the new machinery.

During the nineteenth century carpet making began to boom in the town, with hardwearing Herdwick yarn proving to be an essential ingredient. The Kent Carpet Factory at the top of Burneside Road is now disused but was one of the first mills in Kendal to make carpets.

With child labour laws operating quite differently back then, it was common for children as young as nine or ten to work alongside their fathers, winding spools and learning the trade, and young children had the 'advantage' of being small enough to squeeze into tight spaces beneath looms and, unfortunately, accidents were commonplace.

The Kent Carpet Factory.

Today's Traders

Wool isn't just a part of Kendal's past, it's still very much present today, with modern traders taking over the reins and continuing Kendal's woollen story. Places such as Wools of Cumbria Carpets, a family business that has grown grew from a successful Herdwick wool-spinning business. Present owner Charles Barraclough's father, John, saw an opportunity to use Herdwick wool to make carpets, so he used his contacts in the industry and started off with two different grades of Herdwick (light and dark) and one of Swaledale. He kept the natural colours of the fleeces and although they all had different features, they were all equally hardwearing.

Whilst not all stages of the manufacturing process take place in Cumbria, they do all take place in the north, from Bradford, to Chorley, to Rochdale, with everything being made in small batches from small suppliers. The lovely thing about the shop is that they also sell products from other local wool producers, under the name 'Cumbria Wool Shed' where you'll find everything from covered notepads and cushions from Laura's Loom to hand-tufted rugs from the Woolly Rug Company in Ambleside.

Wools of Cumbria Carpets.

5
The Yarn: How Is Fleece Turned into Yarn?

Let's start with the basic process before we explore the history of yarn production in Cumbria. The fleece needs to go through several steps as it is transformed into yarn. These days most steps in the process have been automated, but in the past they would all have been done by hand. This is a general overview of what's involved:

Shearing
The first step is to shear the fleece from the sheep. Shearing is typically done in the spring to remove the winter fleece and keep the sheep comfortable during warmer months.

Skirting and Sorting
After shearing, the fleece is skirted and sorted. Skirting involves removing any soiled or undesirable parts of the fleece, such as stained or heavily soiled sections. The remaining fleece is then sorted based on its quality, fibre length, and other characteristics.

Sheep shearing.

The sorted fleece is thoroughly washed to remove dirt, grease (lanolin), and other impurities. If you touch a fleece before it has been washed you will feel the waxy residue of lanolin on your hands. The fleece is then gently agitated to loosen dirt and oils, then rinsed multiple times to ensure cleanliness.

Carding

Carding is the next step, which involves aligning the fibres and removing any remaining tangles or impurities. Carding can be done using hand carders or mechanical carding machines. Hand carders are paddle-shaped tools with wire teeth that are used to separate and align the fibres manually. These days mechanical carding machines perform the same task on a larger scale. The result of carding is a continuous web of fibres called a rolag.

Carding the yarn would have been a long and laborious process when done by hand, so it's no surprise that automated carding mills caught on and there are few great examples in Cumbria. Greta carding mill near Keswick was set up in 1638 by Sir John Banks – he left £30 in his will for the mill to be set up to employ 'the poor of the town of Keswick'. The mill later changed to pencil production and is now privately owned accommodation.

Spinning

Next up comes spinning. This is the process of transforming the carded fibres into yarn. Traditionally, spinning was done using a spinning wheel, but today, various methods and machines are used. In spinning, the fibres are drawn out and twisted to create a continuous thread. The degree of twist determines the characteristics of the yarn, such as its strength and drape.

Plying

Once the yarn is spun, it can be plied if desired. Plying involves twisting multiple strands of yarn together to create a thicker, stronger yarn. Plying can be done using a spinning wheel or a machine. After plying, the yarn may undergo additional finishing processes, such as washing, setting the twist, or dyeing, depending on the desired final product.

It's important to remember that today different fibres, such as those from different animals or synthetic materials, are commonly mixed together and may need variations in the specific processes used.

By 1750 there were already nine major types of wool from different breeds of sheep and thirty-nine different grades identified, each with its own purpose:

- Six wools went to the hosiery manufacturers
- Sixteen to the worsted manufacturers (who used the yarn specifically for suits and clothing)
- Seventeen to the coarse wool trade

These trades would have been spread across the county and one record from 1774 noted that in Ambleside there was 'much employed in knitting stockings for Kendal market, in spinning woollen yarn and in making threads to weave their linseys'. (Linesys are fabrics made with a mix of linen and wool and were popular through to the nineteenth century.

Award-winning fleeces.

The wool added warmth to the linen, making it popular with the poor, and it was often used in undergarments and dresses.)

Transportation

John Ireland, who managed Stramongate Mill during the eighteenth century went to Hawkshead market each week to buy 'garn' (as it was known locally). This supply was so important to him that during the 'great frost' of 1785 he had the yarn brought over on sledges to keep his weavers in work.

The smaller fellside weavers would typically buy their wool from 'wool-badgers' who were the middlemen between weavers and the farmers.

The yarn that John bought in Hawkshead would have come from the local valleys and even as far away as the Duddon Valley and Dunmail Raise. As well as buying yarn from across Cumbria, larger weavers would also have 'imported' yarn from Lancashire and Yorkshire and would even have been able to buy in the softer yarns from Leicestershire and Warwickshire. Much of this would have been transported by road making use of our beautiful fell ponies. There is a panel in the Quaker Tapestry in Kendal that captures the ponies carrying wool and cloth to market.

Woolpacks

'The Woolpack' is a common name for pubs and inns in the county, but what exactly is a woolpack, and how is it made? A record from 1851 describes how wool merchants would send their own staff and equipment to weigh and pack wool bought from farmers.

The equipment taken by the wool merchants included a sheet that was around 8 feet long and open on one side, which would have been hung up in the barn. One man weighed the fleeces, and these were then taken into the woolpack where they were trampled into tight layers, alternating across then along the pack. When the pack was full, the edges of the sheet were pulled together then permanently sewn with a pack needle. A full pack contained 240 lbs of wool.

Wild Fell ponies.

Packhorse bridge, Grasmere.

Standard measuring plaque, Ulverston.

These packs would then have been loaded onto wagons and transported around the county, a process that contributed to the many beautiful packhorse bridges we all admire today.

Ensuring fair measurement wasn't always easy. To try and address this, standard measuring plaques would be incorporated into important buildings; there is an excellent example of one from 1875 on the old police station in Ulverston. The history of standardised weights and measures in the UK is surprisingly long and complex and merits a book in its own right, but just to add here that although we see the metric system as being something new, the Weights and Measures (Metric System) Act came into force in 1896.

Historical Dyeing

At this time, the dyeing process could have happened at one of three stages: while it was still a fleece, when it had been turned into thread ready for weaving, or once a garment had been finished.

There is formal evidence of dyeing taking place in Cumbria going back to 1310 when the will of William de Ros lists among his assets a dye house valued at 5s a year. The dyeing process also left its mark on the landscape with a few very pretty 'Dyers Becks' scattered around, such as the one running from Lazonby Hall down into the River Eden near Penrith. The location of this one is no surprise as the local lord owned the dye house and tenants would have paid a fee for its use. They would typically have been located next to the streams as water was an important part of the process.

Regarding colours, a stock list from 1575 includes the following (all original spellings): browne blew, blew and blacke, sky culler, green, gilloflower, contre russet, purple, black redd, and the rather curiously titled sad new culler. Many of these colours would have reflected requirements for official garments.

The colours would have come largely from natural materials; woad and saffron from Somerset and Lincolnshire, madder imported from Brazil coming via Southampton and, more locally, there is evidence of dyer's greenweed and dyer's rocket being collected

Dyer's Beck, St Thomas Church, Kendal.

Natural dyes.

locally. Although dyer's greenwood is now more abundant, at one time it's popularity as a dye source led to scarcity. An account by botanist John Knapp from 1829 notes how it was harvested, often by women, but that 'Greediness … ruined the trade, the plant becoming so injured and stunted by repeated pullings as to be no longer an object worth seeking for'.

In the eighteenth century the colours available boomed with more imports and advances in dye manufacturing. In 1775 a cartel of the five main dye houses in Kendal offered fixed prices on thirty colours including six shades of blue and more exotic options including mazarine (blue) and pompadour (purple). One of the members of the group was George Braithwaite, who bought a yard in Kendal that was dedicated to dry salting – the production of dyes. Today the yard is known as Dr Manning's Yard and it has remained largely unchanged.

After a huge revolution in the chemical dyeing process we have now come full circle, with many producers now returning to 'eco-friendly' dyes.

Traditional Dyeing Today

Today there are smaller mills and dyers scattered around the area. Colourworks in Lancaster is a great example, tucked away in the tiny Covered Yard just off King's Street. In there you'll find Ginette MacDonald, who dyes yarns using methods that our ancestors would be familiar with – the only noticeable difference being that today we can use kettles and urns to heat water, whereas they would have had to rely on fires.

Dyeing yarn takes time and presents many challenges when it comes to creating consistent colours. The process begins with the yarn being soaked for two hours to open up the fibres, before then being heated in a bath of mordant (a metallic salt that helps the yarn to take up the dye) and cream of tartare, which keeps the wool soft. Historically, alum, which forms part of the mordant, used to be imported from Italy until Henry VIII upset the pope, at which point we had to start making our own. There's a great example of an old alum works over near Robin Hood's Bay in Yorkshire.

Dye-soaked yarn.

Dyed yarn.

After cooling overnight Ginette rinses the yarn then adds the dye, with natural ingredients such as nadder being used for red, weld for yellow, walnut husks for browns and fustic (dyers' mulberry) for yellows. Not only does the colour vary depending on how long the yarn is dyed for, what the base yarn type is, etc., but it also varies according to the condition of the natural dyes – growing conditions, how the plant was processed or stored, etc. Once all of that has happened then the yarn has one final bath in a colour modifier to make the colours 'pop' (using washing soda) or 'sadden' (creating subdued shades using iron).

Dyeing using indigo is a whole other process, and a hugely temperamental one at that. The thing that is most impressive is how our ancestors discovered all of this and all the stages that yarn needed to go through before it was ready to work with. It's also a reminder for all of us to think twice next time we think a pretty skein of hand-dyed yarn is a bit expensive...

Spinning

Traditional yarn spinning has changed little over the years and the familiar spinning wheels would have been a common sight in most Cumbrian farmhouses, as would handlooms to turn the yarn into cloth. Yarn and cloth production would have been a very localised affair, produced on the farms and sold in the local markets.

In the Middle Ages, due to the level of financial investment required to build mills and maintain the watercourses, the first industrial spinning and fulling mills were built by the monasteries and lords of the manor. Watermills were popular for the obvious reason that the Lake District generally has plenty of water, so the reason we can take so many picturesque photos of mills next to streams is because that was their only source of power.

The Industrial Revolution shifted spinning to the towns, centralising it and ramping up the volumes that could be produced. In the late eighteenth century woollen mills began

Yarn being spun on spinning wheel.

to spring up around the county. Haithwaites Green Woollen Mill, around 3 miles north of Millom, was one of the earliest woollen manufacturing sites in Cumbria. As well as spinning, weaving, and fulling, bleaching and dyeing also took place there. The mill closed in 1935 and was last heard of being used as a home for hens, but the carding machine was considered so important that it was taken to the Science Museum in London.

Sourcing the Perfect Yarn

If you're looking to work with British yarns today but don't know where to start, then Dr Zoe Fletcher at The Wool List has the answers. Having completed a four-year PhD at Manchester School of Art, she has documented all seventy-two pure British sheep breed and has worked with everyone from farmers to designers and crafters to create The Wool List, which offers a 'Designers Toolkit' of knowledge detailing all you need to know about the fleeces, the breed, and their uses.

Today some local shops still focus on traditionally made, locally sourced yarns. Kate at Northern Yarns in Lancaster turned her lifelong passion for knitting into a flourishing small business that started with a market stall, before evolving into her shop in the heart of the city. Kate's mission is to see just how local she can keep things, with 'wool miles' being kept to a minimum. Her shop specialises in sourcing local yarns produced using traditional methods, and she works directly with farmers, buying and processing in small batches, and specifically focuses on those who are working sensitively with the environment.

6

The History of Hand-knitting

It's possible that knitting has been practised for many hundreds, even thousands, of years, but the problem is that the garments themselves would have long perished. What's more likely to have survived are knitting needles, or sticks, as these would have been made from things like bone. Thee problem with this, however, is that when you find a stick made of bone, how could you prove that it was used for knitting?

Socks

The Victoria and Albert Museum in London has a fascinating collection of ancient woollens, including a pair of red socks, knitted 'in the round' and dating back to around the fourth century. They were found by John de Monins Johnson who was, no doubt, hoping to discover treasures from the Pharaos when he went in hunt of Egyptian treasures, rather than socks. Technically the socks weren't knitted, or crocheted, they were made by nålebinding, which involves 'sewing' together loops using short lengths of yarn.

Other early examples of nålebinding come from Scandanavia where the technique was used to make fishing nets (knit, net, knot, all stemming from a word meaning to bind, twist or tie), and evidence of Viking 'knitted' items have been found across northern Europe.

Socking knitted in the round with double-pointed needles (DPNs).

Closer to home is the 'Coppergate Sock' – a woollen 'sock' discovered on an archaeological dig at Coppergate near York. It looks more like a simple slipper than a modern sock and is the only example of nålebinding to have been discovered in this country. It's worn in places and not 100 per cent intact, but for something that's over 1,000 years old, it looks pretty good.

Early hand-knitters often used knitting sticks – hand-carved sticks made from wood, bone, quill, ivory, or metal wires. These sticks served as supports for knitting needles, especially when working on intricate projects and were often highly treasured possessions, being both practical and often ornate. They were essential for maintaining tension and stability while creating fabric and there are some lovely examples of knitting sticks on the top floor of Farfield Mill, near Sedbergh.

You'll also notice that most early knitting refers to socks, stockings, etc., or 'knitting in the round' – using four needles to create a tube structure. Obviously, this is still very much practised today, but these days knitting flat is generally more commonplace and many knitters find knitting in the round more challenging.

Farfield Mill.

Knitting in the round on circular needles.

Knitting in England

We can't be 100 per cent certain precisely when knitting as we know it today arrived in England. An Oxford inventory from 1320 lists two pairs of 'caligae de Wyrstede' (gaiters) for 11½d. They are described in *A History of Agriculture and Prices in England* (Thorold Rogers) as appearing to be knitted items, although this is far from being conclusive proof. We do know that a technique known as 'sprang' was a popular early method akin to knitting. It comprised of loosely weaving fabrics together to make girdles or stockings, so the fact that these are gaiters could also suggest they were 'knitted'.

Towards the end of the Middle Ages, we have much more concrete evidence of knitting. In 1488 an Act by Henry VII set the price of knitted woollen caps at 2s 8d; for such an Act to have taken place, there must have already been an established knitting trade. Later, we have evidence that Edward IV owned a number of knitted items and there are records showing that Henry VIII's sister, Princess Mary, was gifted two pairs of 'knitte hose'.

One account suggests that in 1564 a gentleman named William Riley saw, in the shop of an Italian merchant, a pair of knitted worsted stocking from Mantua. He borrowed them and made a pair exactly like them, which were reputed to be the first stockings of woollen yarn knitted in England, and they were worn by the Earl of Pembroke. Knitted stockings existed here prior to that as an Act of 1552 covering 'knitte hose' demonstrates, so the William Riley story is interesting but not entirely accurate.

Legislation

The evolution of knitting in this country has been closely related not only to changes in fashion, but also changes in legislation and setting the prices was a way to support the income of the poor; in 1533 Sir Thomas L'Estrange wrote: 'She that sytteth knyttinge from morning to eve, can scarcely win her bread.'

Knitting sticks. (Photo courtesy of Farfield Mill)

A View of Patterdale, John Rathbone, 1788.

    The Cappers Act of 1571 required that every adult in England over the age of six (except for noble folks) wore woollen hats on Sundays and holidays, and failure to do so would result in a 3 farthing fine, which was considered a steep fine at that time. This Act ensured that woollen hats were much in demand which, in turn, provided plenty of work for those making them.

In 1699 as the growth of America boomed and the colonial settlers began to create their own wool industry, Willian III passed an Act that aimed to force them to import British wool, ban them from exporting their own wool, and raise taxes on any sales of wool – an act that so upset our American cousins that it is said by some to have been one of the starting points of the unrest that eventually led to the American Revolution.

Workers

In the 1770s it was estimated that in Kendal alone there were 120 wool combers. Each wool comber supplied five spinners, who each made enough yarn for four to five knitters. In total, there were between 2,000 and 3,000 knitters employed full time in worsted knitting in Kendal, and they produced 6,600 pairs of stockings per week, or 343,000 pairs each year – that's a rate of 2.75 pairs of stockings each, every week.

Of course, the main reason that knitting grew so rapidly up here was the abundance of the raw materials on the doorstep, coupled with the boom in lead mining. The lead mining led to a boom in the local population, but that wasn't the only impact it had on knitting. Because mining lead provided inconsistent employment, knitting filled the gaps when people weren't needed in the mines, and knitting had the advantage that it could be picked up and put down at any time, with no detriment to the item being created.

Gooseholme, Kendal, with tenterframes.

Hand-knitting vs Machine Knitting

In 1589 a gentleman by the name of William Lee from Nottinghamshire invented the first stocking loom, but, due to a long series of unfortunate events, it was nearly 100 years before it had any significant impact on hand-knitting and, even when frame knitting became more popular, it still co-existed alongside hand-knitting throughout the seventeenth century.

Hand-knitting was still able to compete with frame knitting, mainly due to changes in fashion that demand changes in design. This was quick and easy to accomplish for hand knitters, with a few tweaks of a pattern, but was much more problematic for the early knitting machines. However, one major impact on knitting in Cumbria during this period occurred when the British army switched from knee breeches (which required long stockings) to long trousers (which didn't). Undeterred, the local knitters switched from making socks to making sailor's jerseys and caps.

Guilds of knitters were formed where entry was strictly guarded and with long apprenticeships and tough final assessments before membership was granted. These guilds produced the most exquisite, knitted items for the upper echelons of society and ownership would have had much the same kudos as top designer labels have today.

The popularity of hand-knitting continued and demand for goods increased, but after a brief boom it was this demand that eventually led to the downfall the domestic industry. By 1830 demand for dales' hand-knitted items increased so much that suppliers struggled to keep pace, and in 1835 it was reported that wages for knitting increased 30 per cent in just two months. The increase in prices and challenges of meeting demand led to an increased focus on mechanised production in the towns and cities.

Loom shuttle.

By the late nineteenth century production declined dramatically. In *Wensleydale Rambles: A Guide to Picturesque Scenery and Objects of Antiquity* (1878), author J. Routh comments that 'since the invention of machinery and its adoption for purpose of manufacture the hosiery knitters of Wensleydale have either been thrown out of employment or been obliged to work for extremely low wages'. And it would have been a similar story across what is now Cumbria as well and, of course, this fall in demand would have also impacted on the spinners, weavers and dyers too, all of whom were now facing competition from mass production.

As hand-knitting as a form of employment dwindled, so knitting for pleasure and entertainment grew. Those living in the valleys on a limited income would not have had the time or disposable income to spend on knitting as a simple pastime, and so it moved up the economic ladder and became something that young ladies needed to learn – Queen Victoria was famously fond of knitting, with one photograph from the Royal Collection showing her knitting quietly while her youngest daughter reads to her from the newspaper.

An account from 1867 may make many knitters many smile:

It [hand-knitting] may be so easily acquired, even by children, as to be considered almost an amusement. It does not interrupt discourse, distract the attention, or check the powers of imagination. Knitting does no injury to either the body or to the mind. It occasions no prejudicial or injurious position; requires no straining eyesight; and can be performed with much convenience when standing or walking, as when sitting.

This change in the status of knitting naturally had an impact on the local industries surrounding it, which in turn impacted the towns and communities. The tougher yarns

Kendal weavers, 1636.

produced by local sheep such as Herdwicks can't be produced at the scale required by modern clothing manufacturers and are far less favoured than the softer fleeces of the merino, meaning that fleeces that once fetched the best prices at market now cost more to remove than they will ever sell for.

The Wool Story Today

Thankfully there are some local enterprises that are stepping in create a demand for the fleeces again.

The Herdy Company, based in Kendal, do a huge amount to support local farming communities, and one initiative is the Herdy Sleep mattress. They work with ten farms and buy the entire 'clip' of fleeces directly from the farmers at higher rates than they would get elsewhere, with the aim of generating a sustainable income for them. Their initiative has won praise from both the CEO of the Wool Board, who recognised how Herdy have contributed to the increased awareness of the Herdwick breed and its many uses, and The Worshipful Company of Woolmen.

Cable and Blake, also based in Kendal, began in 2016 when upholsterer Rachel Cabble and her partner Alice began creating a range of stunning fabrics using Herdwick fleeces. Designing hardwearing fabrics was never going to be enough for them though, they needed to be beautiful too, so they experimented with different dyes and colourways to create a breathtaking range that currently includes thirteen colourways and seven different designs.

Herdwick ram, Eskdale.

Cable & Blake upholstery. (With thanks to Cable & Blake for the image)

Once they had the fabrics they got to work producing home furnishings, including lampshades and cushions as well as upholstering furniture, which can be seen in places such as the Michelin-starred restaurant L'Enclume, but they didn't stop there. Today twenty-one local craftspeople use their fabrics to create bespoke items such as handbags, scarves and even miniature Herdwicks, which are then sold in the shop – reflecting the way that communities worked together in the past.

7
The History of British Wool Exports Around the World

For centuries, the British Isles have been renowned for their wool industry, with woollen goods serving as a vital commodity that influenced economies and cultures around the world.

The Romans thought very highly of British wool and used it to make hard-wearing rugs and capes which were then exported around their empire. Elsewhere in the country the first ever factory in Britain was built near Winchester by the Romans to weave cloth, with a dye works believed to have existed at nearby Silchester.

The Vikings also made good use of the local wool; longships in Norway have been discovered to have sails made from wool, which would have required in the region of 500 fleeces to make.

The Woolsack in the House of Lords is where the Lord Speaker sits. It is a large, square cushion which, in 1938, was restuffed with wool from Britain and all the nations of the Commonwealth. It first appeared in the fourteenth century and is a mark of how important the international woold trade was to the country at that time.

Fulling Mill location, Sourmilk Gill, Easedale.

While Cumbria may have produced many thousands of fleeces during this time, the ports of Whitehaven and Barrow probably played very little role in the trade. Back then the towns were no more than tiny fishing villages and there is no evidence of major trading; however, the significant Roman presence at places such as Ravenglass would suggest that it is likely that they made some use of the local coast for trade. The Romans were famed for their road systems, however, so this is probably a more likely route for wool to have been moved and traded, both around the country and internationally.

The Value of Wool

At one time wool was so valuable that it was used instead of money, and in 1194 it was English fleeces that paid the ransom for Richard the Lionheart. But, as with all good things, this golden era for English wool exports came to an end when during the thirteenth century the Spanish emerged onto the market with the merino sheep, whose fine fleece was softer but still offered the same levels of warmth as the hardier English breeds.

Merino sheep are not suited to the British climate, so breeding them here was not an option and, to start with a least, it was illegal to bring them here. For several centuries, exports of the breed were not allowed, and anyone caught trying to do so, could face the death penalty.

Herdwicks feeding on hay.

Wool was so central to the national economy that in 1294, in order to fund the war with France, the English government levied a tax of 3 marks on every bag of wool. This was not popular and became known as the 'maltolt' (bad tax). Wool merchants and other producers protested against the tax, and it was retracted in 1297.

When the fleece export industry fell into decline the realisation came that instead of exporting fleeces to weavers abroad, England should make its own cloths and fabrics to export alongside and, eventually instead of, fleeces. In the early fourteenth century, due to unrest in the Low Countries Edward III invited a number of Flemish weavers to settle in England under his protection. These weavers breathed life into the English weaving industry and by the middle of the fourteenth century England exported around 5,000 pieces of cloth annually – a number that continued to grow dramatically over the next two centuries. The impact of this was that wool replaced corn as the most valuable crop and, with much of Cumbria better suited to sheep than arable farming, this had a major impact on trade in the county.

Of course, there are plenty of people in the county who farm things other than sheep, and Amy Bateman's superb *Forty Farms* book is perfect for anyone wanting to explore the broader picture of farming in Cumbria. That said, out of the forty farms in Amy's book, twenty-six of them farmed sheep, but of those twenty-six only three cited sheep as the only business on their farm – the rest have had to diversify, with tourism, hospitality, and beef farming being the most popular options.

Swaledales, Old St Catherine's Church, Crook.

The Monasteries

The establishment of monastic orders, particularly the Cistercians, played a pivotal role in promoting sheep farming and wool production. Wool was hugely important to the monks at both Furness and Shap abbeys. Their connections to international trade helped to account for the fact that by the late thirteenth century, wool comprised around 50 per cent of England's annual export value, with fleeces going mainly to Italy, Germany and the Low Countries.

Monks would borrow money against the future value of wool, sowing the seeds of what is now the commodities market, and use the profits from the trade to build their magnificent abbeys. If a monastery decided that it required a new wing, for example, but it didn't have the money to hand, it would strike a deal with a cloth trader who might agree to give them a lump sum up front, allowing them to build their new wing, in return for all of the wool for the next ten years.

To meet that demand, it's estimated that Shap Abbey had around 2,000 sheep and Furness Abbey closer to 6,000 – far larger than the flock sizes seen on today's farms. They also made good use of the sheep at home as well; a monk's uniform would typically have been made from hardwearing Herdwick wool. The fleeces from the younger brown lambs were used for the more junior monks, with the lighter fleeces of the older sheep being used for the more senior monks.

Furness Abbey.

Shap Abbey.

Kendal on the World Stage

Just as wool production initially shaped the towns, so cloth production and international trade would now do the same. In 1575 Queen Elizabeth I confirmed Kendal's charter of incorporation, with the charter giving tight control of the fabric industry.

It was during this era that Kendal truly established itself at the heart of the region's wool and fabric production. The fabrics produced were primarily cheaper fabrics for the working classes. In 1590 Kendal was described as 'A place famed for excellent cloathing [sic] and for its remarkable industry'. The town's reputation for fabric production at this time was even memorialised by Shakespeare in *Henry IV Part 1*:

> FALSTAFF: But as the devil would have it, three misbegotten knaves in Kendal green came at my back

It's unlikely that the Bard himself ever visited the county, but the mention of the fabric in his work demonstrates how well known and valued it was.

Prosperous as the cloth trade was, the story was very different for the hill farmers, who saw little of the wealth generated from the international trade. This was because, in a story that is very reminiscent of modern-day trading, the buying and selling of wool was controlled by the Merchant Staplers Company, meaning that the raw wool trade was dominated by a few rich players. James I tried to fix this by designating certain towns as 'staple towns' where wool should be exchanged, and Kendal was named as one of these towns.

River Kent old ford, Kendal.

Kendal coat of arms.

Pedestrian tunnel depicting Kendal's wool heritage.

The problem was that the hill famers were too remote from the town and the traders went after the easier trading areas in the Midlands and the south. By 1618 much of the wool demand from hill farms had dried up and, alongside that, the fulling mills in the valleys vanished too.

By the mid-seventeenth century other countries were getting in on the fabric production scene, including the French, who developed a reputation for producing cheaper cloths of equal quality to those from Cumbria.

At one point international trade was halted by law. James I prohibited the export of wool, with the aim that manufacturers would have a plentiful supply on their doorstep, but as English wool was still in demand abroad, this led to huge incidences of smuggling and the law was eventually repealed in 1624.

Wool and fabric production remained one of Britain's main sources of wealth and, because of that, it enjoyed many privileges thanks to successive governments being keen to support it. As Ephraim Lipson noted in his 1921 book *The History of the Woollen and Worsted Insustries*: 'The government lavished upon it the most unremitting care and attention and created for its protection an elaborate code of industrial and commercial regulations.'

By the close of the eighteenth century there were over 300 laws covering all aspects of the wool and cloth production process.

The Industrial Revolution

As we have already described, the Industrial Revolution had a dramatic impact on the county, but it also lead to vastly increased volumes of cloth production, much of it destined for export. It brought about a surge in demand for wool, leading to the expansion of sheep farming in the region, and this expansion demanded an improved transportation infrastructure, including canals and later railways, to allow the movement of wool from the rural areas to the industrial centres, like Manchester and Leeds. This in turn led to Cumbria's farmers adapting to the changes and embracing selective breeding techniques to produce high-quality wool and meet the rising demands of the textile industry.

Changing modes of transportation.

In the early part of the Industrial Revolution our exports were mainly heading for Europe, but as the nineteenth century dawned our export reach stretched around the globe, thanks in no small part to less savoury parts of our past, including the creation of the Empire. This allowed for export, and import, arrangements to be made with India and even Australia, which began providing wool from the far side of the globe to our textile industry. This trade continues today, and in 2020 the UK imported around £8.5 million worth of Australian fleeces for our textiles industry – these tend to be finer fleeces that can be produced there in very large quantities.

Into the twentieth century British-made garments were well known for their quality and craftsmanship, giving us a competitive edge in a global market, but things were about to shift again. The growth of other industrialised nations and the discovery and proliferation of synthetic fibres had a major impact on local wool production and local textile and fabric production.

Mechanisation has seen the size of the industry decrease in human terms. In 1890 there were over 275,000 people employed in textile production and by 1980 that had dropped to around 50,000, mainly due to international competition.

Today there are somewhere in the region of 88,000 people employed in textile production in the UK and, after many years of decline, the number of UK garment manufacturers increased by 13 per cent in the ten years to 2020 to 4,005.

International markets demand fine, soft fleeces in huge numbers that our coarser native breeds and smaller-scale farming find it hard to compete with. The boom in knitting and crocheting, especially those keen to use natural, local yarns, does help some producers, but it tends to be a localised and specialist industry, with little meaningful ability to take on the international big hitters.

Weaving on a loom.

8

Wool and the Communities

Wool played a crucial role in connecting communities and had a significant social impact in the local area. Wool co-operatives allowed small-scale producers to come together to access broader markets and obtain better prices for their garments.

What for most of us is now a pleasurable pastime, perhaps used to de-stress us after a busy day at work, was once a vital lifeline for remote communities. And at a time when some people were so poor that they tucked themselves up in bed and knitted under the blankets to save on heating, lives literally depending on knitting to bring in enough of an income in order to survive.

In the dales of Cumbria women and children contributed to the family income by carding, spinning and knitting. In Westmorland the coats produced were known as the 'gray-coats of Westmorland'. The *Agricultural Survey of Westmorland* (Pringle, 1794) describes the area as follows: 'Its exports are woollen cloth, manufactured in Kendal, stockings, slates, tanned hides, gunpowder, hoops, charcoal, hams, wool, sheep and cattle.' In 1823 it was estimated that in Swaledale and Wensleydale the yearly value of knitted goods was around £40,000 – that's the equivalent of nearly £5 million today.

But knitting wasn't just the preserve of women. Tom Daley may have done a lot to inspire a new generation of men to pick up their needles and get stuck in, but back in

Kirkby Stephen Stocking Market, 1817.

Mother and daughter.

the nineteenth century knitting in the valleys was seen as something for both sexes, as this report from Revd W. Nicholls in *The History and Traditions of Mallerstang Forest* in 1883 illustrates: 'Knitting was a universal occupation, both for men and women; indeed, it used to be said, when two young folks were 'wed' that if they were both good knitters they would do.' In Budworth's *A Fortnight's Ramble to the Lakes* (1792) he describes how 'Both men and women were knitting stockings as they drove their carts into town [Kendal]'.

And in *The Beauties of England and Wales* from 1814 the following idyllic scene is described: 'the women often carried the dung hotts, a sort of wicker panniers, on their shoulders to the fields, while the men laid in groups on a sunny banks, employed in knitting.'

Knitting Villages

The communities around Ravenstonedale were well known for supplying stockings for the markets in Kendal. In 1801 the population of the village was just 1,138, but they produced 1,000 pairs of stockings every week, with people earning 5s–6s each week from knitting.

As well as being financially important to these distant communities, knitting also brought them together. Knitters used to 'go forth' to each other's homes to knit in groups,

Freshly shorn Herdwick flock ready for spray marking.

chatting, telling stories and even singing knitting songs to match the rhythm of the knitting. Here's an example of a short ditty from Cumberland:

> Bulls at bay
> Kings at fay
> Over the hills and far away

There were longer tunes too. One carding song stretched to five verses and began:

> Oh! tarry woo; oh! tarry woo!
> Tarry woo is ill to spin;
> Oh! card it weel, oh! card it weel,
> Card it weel ere ye begin

A more detailed description of these gatherings can be found in Adam Sedgwick's *A Memorial to Cowgill Chapel* from 1868. Here he describes 'sittings' where groups, including family parties, would gather together around the fire on cold winter evenings. The 'lang settle' was a long bench with a high back that ran from one side of the fireplace; on the other side would be the patriarch's wooden armchair.

Not related to knitting, but amusing for any cat owners, he also describes a 'cat-malison' (meaning cat's curse), which is a small cupboard, tucked up in the rafters, where things of importance were kept, well out of the reach of the cat!

As people arrived, they would take their seats and set about knitting 'with a speed that cheated the eye', making stockings and gloves. As well as singing songs and catching up on all the latest gossip, he describes a scene which anyone who has ever tried to follow a sock or glove pattern will be impressed with, especially when you consider they were working with only the light from the fire and a few candles:

> Or by way of change, some lassie who was bright and renable [talkative] was asked to read for the amusement of the party. She would sit down; and, apparently without interrupting her work by more than a single stitch, would begin to read – for example, a chapter of *Robinson Crusoe*.

Sedgwick paints a nostalgic picture of the events, which were common throughout the valleys, describing them as a place where 'labour and love were for a while united'. Today knitters and crocheters still come together in groups right across the country and many even join in virtual events via Zoom. Ethel & Em, a popular yarn store in Lancaster, started up virtual 'Knit, Knot and Natter' events during the pandemic and they are still very popular – probably because no one is required to read *Robinson Crusoe* aloud while they work!

Over in Orton, in 1795, most women were employed in knitting stockings for the Kendal markets, and in 1868 it was reported that six elderly knitters in the village had a combined age of 478 years, but still managed to produce seventy-two pairs of stockings each month.

The Markets

The Stocking Market in Kirkby Stephen was another important trade opportunity for knitters. In 1777 it was described as 'a considerable market town noted for the sale of a great number of stockings knit there and in the neighbourhood'. An illustration of this market from 1817 is interesting for many reasons, not least of which is the group of women, gathered in one corner, clearly wearing their finest skirts and bonnets, and engaged deeply in conversation.

Today we take instant communication for granted, but back then these markets would have provided more than simply an income, important as that was. These events provided a much-needed opportunity to meet up and exchange news and knitting tales. Members of today's modern-day knitting groups and communities will attest to the importance of chatting to someone about a troublesome pattern, a yarn that won't behave itself, or that one stitch that you just can't seem to get right.

Although each of these groups were working on a small scale, when the Industrial Revolution happened and production was centralised, creating cheaper garments on a vast scale, the impact of the loss of income on these smaller communities was huge. It led to the depopulation of many areas, as people moved towards towns and cities.

Bretherdale Head bridge.

Bretherdale Head abandoned farm.

If you want to see an abandoned village then Bretherdale Head, just north of Kendal, is a fascinating example. It has the feel of a ghost town, with homes and buildings simply abandoned. It also has an interesting connection to the woollen industry as a very rare shield-shaped weight dating back to the fourteenth century was found at a farm there. It would have originally been used by one of the king's tax collectors assessing the wool tax in the area.

Bretherdale Head outbuilding.

Guilds

It is thought that spinning, knitting and weaving guilds date back to medieval times; for example, the weavers guild in York was first recorded in 1163 when members each had to pay the king £10 a year for the privilege of being a member. That may not sound like much, but it equates to something in the region of £16,000 today, demonstrating that the guilds were very much the preserve of the monied gentry.

These guilds were initially formed by skilled artisans seeking to protect their trade secrets and maintain high standards of craftsmanship. The Industrial Revolution brought both challenges and opportunities to these guilds as mechanisation transformed the textile industry. While some struggled to adapt, others embraced innovation and incorporated knitting machines into their practises.

Historically the guilds would have provided an opportunity for traders to buy and sell wool and associated garments, with a strong commercial focus. Today, many local craft guilds still exist, but the focus has shifted to preserving skills, sharing expensive equipment, and connecting with like-minded people. Modern local guilds also do a huge amount of work connecting with others in the community to encourage a younger generation to get involved and promote skills through a variety of workshops and organised courses.

In the days before there was a national currency, local guilds even created their own currency of small coins, which members were obliged to take and later exchange for silver. Kendal Guild issued nine different coins, with most designs relating to wool industry.

Kendal had its own guild, but, whereas Preston Guild continues on its twenty-one-year cycle, the final Kendal Guild procession took place on 4, 5 and 6 June 1759. A man on horseback rode through the town dressed as Bishop Blaise (the patron saint of wool combers), he was followed by 100 local wool combers as well as 300 weavers, 80 shearmen and dyers, 150 tailors, 100 shoemakers, 80 ironmongers, 60 tanners, 100 builders and 70 glovers.

Hand weaving wool rugs.

Kendal Town Hall.

As they marched, they sang the long guild song which had a separate verse for each occupation, and began with this:

> Kendal long famed for trade and useful arts,
> Sends forth her skilful sons with joyful hearts,
> Clothed with the product of their native land,
> Wrought with the labour of each artist's hands,
> In ordered rank they march with solemn pace,
> With music, flags and every martial grace.

Modern-day Co-operatives

Today there are a number of modern-day co-operatives that have come together to enable local skilled crafters to share skills and work together profitably. In Cumbria we have a great example of this with The Wool Clip, based in Priest's Mill, Calbeck, in the north of the county. They were born out of the Foot and Mouth epidemic of 2001 after the disease affected over half the farms in the county.

Just months after the footpaths reopened, and with many farming families still reeling from the impact, The Wool Clip first opened their doors and within two months they were hitting their targets. The central theme that guides them is 'adding value to

Priest's Mill, Calbeck.

The Wool Clip.

wool' and their Aladdin's cave shop shows off every aspect of wool production, from fleeces to looms, yarns, fabrics and finished clothing items. Their fourteen members, including people involved at every stage of the production, including farmers, and their not-for-profit ethos means that the community is central to everyone involved, and this includes ensuring that personal well-being is just as important as the items they produce.

In the same way that the historic co-operatives and communities came together in a farmhouse kitchen warmed by the heat of the fire, so today's communities still come together, albeit in different ways and often aided by technology. The way they connect may be different, but the reasons for that connection remain as important as they ever were.

9
The Patterns

Patterned knitting.

Fabric patterns have played a significant role throughout history, carrying cultural, social, and artistic significance. These are just a few of the historical significances that are associated with fabric patterns:

Cultural Identity
These have long been used to express and reinforce cultural identities. Different regions and communities have developed distinct patterns that reflect their unique traditions, beliefs, and history, as we saw in Chapter 1 with shepherd's plaid.

Status and Wealth
In England, certain fabric patterns were reserved for the elite or the ruling class, symbolising wealth, power, and social status.

In the thirteenth century, sumptuary laws in the UK were established to control and limit the clothing choices of various social classes. These regulations aimed to preserve the social hierarchy by ensuring that only the affluent could afford luxurious and fashionable garments.

Traditional garment making.

The earliest known sumptuary law in England was an ordinance from the City of London in 1281, which set rules for workers' attire. The purpose of these laws was to curb excessive spending on clothing and to stop commoners from mimicking the appearance of the aristocracy. Violating these laws could lead to severe penalties, including fines and property confiscation. By dictating what people could wear, sumptuary laws reinforced social distinctions and helped maintain the existing class structure.

Historical Events and Movements
Fabric patterns have occasionally gained historical significance due to their association with important events or social movements. For example, during the American Revolution, homespun fabrics with simple patterns became symbols of resistance to British taxation and the quest for independence.

Fashion and Style
Fabric patterns have played a crucial role in fashion and style trends throughout history and continue to do so today.

Trade and Globalisation
The spread of fabric patterns has often been connected with trade routes and globalisation. Patterns from one region would influence and be adopted by others through trade and cultural exchange, leading to the cross-pollination of design elements and styles.

Knitting pattern ready to go!

Symbol of Resistance

In some instances, fabric patterns have been adopted as symbols of resistance or political movements. For example, in the eighteenth century, following the Jacobite uprising, the British government enacted the Dress Act of 1746, which prohibited the wearing of tartan and other elements of Highland dress to suppress Scottish culture and identity. The prohibition lasted for thirty-six years, making the wearing of tartan an act of defiance and a symbol of Scottish resistance during this time. When the ban was lifted in 1782, tartan re-emerged as a powerful symbol of Scottish heritage and pride.

Kendal Pattern Book

The story of the discovery of the Kendal Pattern Book is almost as exciting as the information it contains.

The book was discovered by chance by a refuse collector named Jimmy Rigg who was sorting through wastepaper from Kendal Castle Mills during the Second World War. He thought it had some sort of historical significance so saved it from destruction and passed it on to a local historian named Jack O'Connor. In 1951 Mr O'Connor passed it

The 1769 Kendal Pattern Book. (Photo taken with kind permission of Kendal Town Council)

Inside the front cover of the original Kendal Pattern Book. (Photo taken with kind permission of Kendal Town Council)

on to Kendal Town Hall where it remained, being freely handled by curious staff and visitors, until 1984.

The book was then passed to another local historian who brought it to the attention of the Victoria and Albert Museum in London. They determined that the book was from the late eighteenth century (there is a date of 1769 on the inside cover) and although it contained some rare examples of high-end patterned fabrics, what makes the book so unique is that it also includes many examples of coarse, ordinary cloths worn by the lower classes, which were of even greater interest as these types of clothing samples were very rarely preserved.

It was most likely a book that would have been taken to Kendal market to be shown to townsfolk and local farmer's wives so that they could select clothing fabrics. The book was prepared for conservation, and, during that process, a few samples were taken which give an insight into the dyeing processes and composition of the dyes, as well as the construction of the fabrics.

The book itself is fairly hefty and although it only has twenty leaves, these are bound between boards, with the whole tome bound in dark brown leather. In total there are

505 cloth samples mounted, although seven are missing. The breakdown of fabrics is as follows:

Linen and worsted	203
Linen and woollen	153
Linen, worsted and woollen	114
Linen, worsted and silk	3
Linen, worsted and cotton	10
Worsted and silk	15
Total	498

There were twenty-nine samples of wool taken from the book, which showed four different fleece types, from coarser hairy fleeces through to finer ones. Whilst there was no evidence of fine imported yarns such as merino, there was also no evidence of our native Herdwicks either. Although some of the yarns had been plyed (two spun strands then spun and twisted together), none of them had been blended (mixed prior to spinning).

What this suggests is that although there was an ample supply of local sheep, the hosiers of Kendal often brought in yarn from other sources. A ledger from the late eighteenth century shows yarn being brought in from Northumberland, Leicestershire, Staffordshire, Warwickshire and Yorkshire, in addition to local yarns from Kendal, Troutbeck, Allonby, and Ulverston.

One of the most exciting elements of the book was the analysis of the dyes, showing how they were made and the colours on offer in a period before the widespread use of synthetic dyes:

Blue: All the blue samples contained indigotin derived either from indigo or woad and both were regularly used in England in the eighteenth century.
Red: Madder, from the root of Rubia tinctorum, was the most widely used and records show that it was mostly imported from the Netherlands.
Yellow: This came from alum and tin.
Green: All the green dyes tested contained different components but were a mix of yellow and blue. The analysis also showed the presence of genistein, the main colourant from dyer's greenweed.
Purple: This came from mixing red and blue, but some of the purples were also obtained from lichen, which is especially interesting as it was unusual to see lichen purple used by itself during this period.
Blacks and browns: These came from a mixture of using successive dyeings using the heavy shades of red, yellow and blue, which was effective but expensive.

The name inside the cover of the book is John Crewdson. His family can trace their Kendal lineage right back to 1575, which was the year Kendal town was granted its charter of incorporation by Elizabeth I. They were also a family who liked to name their

Textile samples with stock numbers. (Photo taken with kind permission of Kendal Town Council)

sons 'John' so it's not all that easy to figure out which one of them the book belonged to, although it most likely belongs to the one born in 1726. His father (also called John) was born in 1701 and was one of Kendal's principal merchants, employing over 700 people in woollen manufacture.

When it was discovered, the book was already well worn, which probably explains why it had been thrown away, and years of being handled didn't do it much good either. By the time the North West Museums Service received it to conserve it, the front cover was detached and the spine was split. The cover in general was dirty and covered with the wax and grease from the hundreds of hands it had passed through, and the corners were all scuffed and worn.

Thankfully they did an excellent job and the book remains at Kendal Town Hall. It can be viewed by appointment via the Town Council website (kendaltowncouncil.gov.uk) and is on display during special events.

However well preserved the book is, the colours will have inevitably faded over the years, but, thanks to a painstaking project by the Lancs and Lakes Guild of Weavers, Spinners and Dyers, we now have an idea of how it may originally have looked. They have completely reproduced the book and all the patterns it contains, in perfect eye-popping colour, and have even gone so far as to weave enough fabric to recreate a dress from the era as well.

It was a major undertaking involving a surprising amount of maths as they translated the original patterns into something they could recreate on looms today. The project took over a year, with eighteen members of the guild working tirelessly to recreate the book.

Wear and tear on the original pattern book. (Photo taken with kind permission of Kendal Town Council)

Kendal's coat of arms on the Town Hall: *Pannus Mihi Panis*.

Their reproduction enabled them not only to understand more about how the original book was put together, but also to preserve those patterns and techniques for future generations to enjoy.

Dot dot, dash dash

Knitting patterns have also played an important role in our more recent history. During the war, knitting provided a means for sending coded messages, with knitters creating patterns of knit and purl stitches to send Morse code signals hidden in their garments, something that created enough of a stir that America's Office of Censorship passed legislation that banned knitting patterns from being posted abroad in case they contained sensitive information. This sounds pretty straightforward but, having tried it, it does require surprisingly large garments as each letter is made up of several dots and dashes.

A less clandestine, but equally important movement was the Knit for Victory campaign which, during both world wars, saw women coming together in groups to knit garments for soldiers on the front line. Often, they would knit for friends or family members, but the groups would also produce items for the front line in general, as well as for hospitals. Special patterns were produced – copies of old books still survive and show a range of basic patterns for socks, jumpers, hats, scarves and mittens.

Cumbrian yarn the wool that binds the county

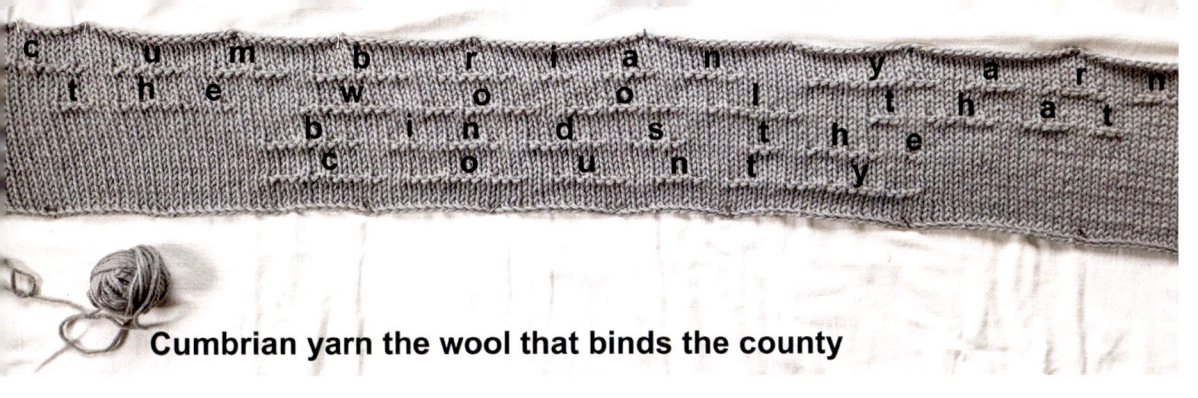

Woollen Morse code.

Herdwick lambs start black then moult to white.

And knitting was so popular that a number of songs sprung up which the women sang as they knitted. Even Glen Miller wrote a song, recorded by Judy Garland, called 'Knit One, Purl Two' which starts out like this:

Knit one, purl two
This sweater, my darling's for you
While vigil, you're keeping through rain and storm
This sweater will keep you warm

10
Important Mills and Farms

As we've seen throughout the book, the woollen industry – from the farms to the markets – has left its mark right across the county. Sometimes it's an obvious mark, but other times less so, which is why this final chapter is dedicated to the mills and farms of the county.

Many of these are still available to visit, some have been preserved in close to their original glory, and others are now private homes with quirky features that interior designers probably love, but the thing they all have in common is that they played an important role in shaping Cumbria as we know it today.

Farfield Mill, Sedbergh

The Dover family were a mix of farmers and woollen manufacturers. Joseph Dover was a force to be reckoned with and took over Heblethwaite Hall Woollen Mill near Cautley in 1812 – sadly only one small section of a wall remains of this mill, but it was once central to the local woollen industry and housed one of the first carding machines in the region.

Farfield Mill, Sedbergh.

He was an astute businessman and operations soon expanded. In 1836 he paid £490 for 9 acres of land on a bend in the River Clough and built Farfield Mill, which opened in 1837 (the same year a young Queen Victoria came to the throne).

The mill was renowned for making linings for horse collars, which they sold locally and exported to Australia – they even supplied cloths to Queen Victoria and, later, Edward VII.

In 1909 a fortuitous disaster struck when the original mill was burned down, but it enabled the owners to rebuild along more modern lines. Unfortunately, not long after that, the Australians began to impose steep taxes on imported cloth and that, together with the rise of the car and decline of domestic horse use, led to a gradual drop in business and the mill was sold in 1937.

It was bought by the Farfield Spinning Company, who made carpet yarn, and it also served as Admiralty stores when it was requisitioned during the Second World War. Thankfully It survived largely intact, and today it is owned and run by Farfield Mill Limited, a charitable community benefit society. The mill is open throughout the year and boasts an excellent array of local artists and creators, a superb café, and a range of original looms and artefacts including a working Dobcross power loom from 1936, and a 300-year-old Witney Blanket Loom from the Industrial Revolution.

Fulling Mill, Ambleside

It is thought that over 500 fulling mills once existed across the county, preparing woollen cloths so that they were ready for tailoring. This number would have dropped dramatically during the Industrial Revolution before dwindling away to zero. The fact that many of them were housed in substantial buildings means that they haven't been lost entirely so we can still see them today, and the old fulling mill in Ambleside is a lovely example.

Today it's home to the Flying Fleece pub in the heart of the town, but many of the original features remain. The present owners have traced the history and identified that it was a fulling mill at least as far back as 1454, when it was one of four local fulling mills. As we have already seen, all woollen roads led to Kendal back then and the fabrics produced here were sent to the markets of Kendal along much the same routes that we'd take today – although there would probably have been a lot less traffic around in those days...

In 1795 the mill was rebuilt as a woollen mill, making hosiery items that were sold through Kendal before the rise of machine-made garments in neighbouring Lancashire led to the inevitable decline of local production. The mill fell into disrepair and the weir was washed away but the unique light and location it offered was recognised and, during the Second World War, the building was home to students from the Royal College of Art.

The mill was finally saved and refurbished in 1990 and today provides a popular stopping-off spot where you can relax away from the bustle of the town and enjoy a quiet drink alongside Stock Gill.

Fulling Mill, Ambleside.

Fulling Mill restored waterwheel.

Millbeck Towers, Keswick

Probably the most impressive of all the old mills we'll visit in this chapter, with its iconic turrets and landscaped surroundings. Today this old carding mill is owned by the National Trust and let out as a holiday rental, with the rooms that once housed machinery now making for large airy living and dining spaces.

The original mill was built in the late eighteenth century and bought by John Daniel Banks in 1903 and, although he had ambitious plans for a *Grand Designs* Swiss chalet-style conversion, he eventually settled on what we now see, with almost all of the original interior features preserved, including lofty ceilings and impressive stained-glass windows.

Millbeck Towers, Keswick.

Dockray Hall Mills, Kendal

This was a collection of mills that is thought to have existed since medieval times and, during the eighteenth century, we know that woollen manufacturing and dyeing took place there. It's quite handy when things go up for sale as it means we have more detailed records, and in 1809 all four mills on the site were put up for sale. The listing records: '1 mill for rasping and chipping dyeing woods; 2 fulling mills with carding room and wool room and a friezing mill.'

The mills at Dockwray were powered by water from the nearby River Kent, which was once dammed near where the railway line crosses Burneside Road. The original mills burned down in 1824, but new mills were built in their place, quoted as being 'the largest manufacturing building ever erected in the county', and the site was home to carpet production up until 1940.

Since then, more of the mills have been demolished, with just a few buildings remaining, including one that is now, in a wonderful loop of history, being used as a carpet warehouse for nearby Kendal Quality Carpets. If you look at the roof of the mill, the tall, flat sections were once all windows to allow for the maximum amount of light to be let in to the mill. With a little detective work you can still spot the old millrace too, leading straight to the old mill.

Sprint Mill, Burneside

Sprint Mill is tucked away in a narrow gorge, on the banks of the River Sprint, in Burneside. Cloth was manufactured on the site at least as far back as the fifteenth century, powered by water from the local stream, and it remained in operation through to 1954.

Despite being one of the oldest surviving mills in the county, the present owners made an interesting discovery when they undertook a major renovation – the mill had been built without any foundations. Fortunately, the renovation was a complete success,

Dockray Hall Mills, Kendal.

the building was preserved and it is now part of National England's Environmental Stewardship Schemes and both the mill, and the 15 acres it sits in, are managed using traditional methods.

The present owners, Romola and Edward Acland, describe it as having '968 panes of glass in the windows ... 565 drawers containing a collection from a bygone age, with cagmagery and bits and pieces galore'. It is now home to Sprintmilling Art who host exhibitions at the site.

The Farms of Beatrix Potter

Hilltop Farm at Near Sawrey may be the first farm that Beatrix Potter bought, and it is the site that gets all the attention and the visitors. It is definitely worth a visit (while you're there also pop into the Tower Bank Arms for a drink – it never disappoints!), but Ms Potter also owned fifteen other farms in the area where she bred and maintained her beloved Herdwicks. Here is just a small selection of those.

Bridge End Farm, Little Langdale

There is evidence of farming in this valley going all the way back to the Vikings and an archaeological report from Oxford Archaeology makes for fascinatingly detailed reading. The buildings and barns we see here today date back to the eighteenth and nineteenth centuries, with Beatrix Potter buying it in 1934. As with many properties, she gifted it to

Bridge End Farm, Little Langdale.

the National Trust after her death and although there are fourteen other farms that were owned by her, none of them have quite as spectacular a setting as this one.

High Yewdale Farm, Coniston

This is an old farm with a modern, all-too-familiar story. The farm dates back to the seventeenth century when sheep farming and the woollen industry was at its peak in Cumbria, and it was bought by Beatrix Potter in 1943. After her death it was managed and run by the National Trust, with a tenant farmer managing a flock of around 1,000 Herdwicks. It was a popular and well-respected farm that enjoyed a visit from Elizabeth II in 1985, who was said to found it a 'marvellous' place.

In 2005, when that farmer reached retirement, the National Trust made the decision to break up the farm and restructure the property, with the land going to adjoining farms and most of the buildings being repurposed as accommodation. They said that the restructuring was in response to the modern-day pressures and requirements of farming, meaning the older, more traditional methods were no longer financially viable.

Yew Tree Farm, Coniston

This is a wonderful old farm that is still very active today. There is a rare and excellent example of an old spinning gallery in the old barn which would have been used for the drying and spinning of Herdwick fleeces produced by the farm.

Today the farm is an active hub, and a great demonstration of how diverse many farms need to be in order to survive. They offer weddings, exhibitions, a fine café, and Herdwick meats, alongside the 'Herdwick Experience' which begins with a talk explaining the background and heritage of the sheep before moving into an exploration of the local farm and landscape. From there it's just a short walk to the fields behind the farm where you

High Yewdale Farm, Coniston.

Yew Tree Farm, Coniston.

begin by feeding a handpicked flock of friendly 'Herdies', before lying on the grass with them as they nuzzle up to you, surrounded by the Coniston fells.

And, if the farm looks familiar, it's because it was used as Hilltop Farm for the 2006 film *Miss Potter*, starring Renée Zellweger.

Troutbeck Park Farm, Troutbeck

After spending several years at Hilltop, Ms Potter was made aware by her husband of a farm and large plot of land that was coming up for sale in the Troutbeck Valley, nestled quietly beneath Kirkstone Pass. When she purchased the 1,875 acres for £8,000 in 1923, she immediately became one of the largest landowners in the county, but her motivation was not to become a property mogul, quite the opposite in fact; she was aware that the land was likely to be sold to developers with a large number of holiday accommodation units planned. She bought the site to save it.

When she first bought it, it already had a tenant farmer – a Mrs Leake who lived there with her two sons – but the farm was somewhat rundown and after three years the Leake family left and Beatrix took over management of the farm, supported by George Walker, the brother-in-law of Tom Storey who ran the Hilltop farm. The house to the right of the main farmhouse was built specifically for him.

She continued to write while she was there, creating a small study to work in, and used the farm as the setting for her Fairy Caravan stories.

A lesser-known fact and something that is controversial today, is that Ms Potter was a big supporter of the local hunt and included a clause in the deeds of the farm that hunting was allowed to continue on her land for all time.

Beatrix Potter has perhaps done more than anyone else when it comes to protecting what we now know as the Lake District landscape and when she died in 1943 her estate was valued at £211, 636 4s 10d, which is just shy of £8 million at today's prices. She's also credited with turning around the fortunes of Herdwick sheep so that we can continue to enjoy their smiley faces and warm, woolly fleeces today.

Troutbeck Park Farm, Troutbeck.

Herdy smiley faces.